INVISIBLE ME

INVISIBLE ME

Edited by
Susanna K. Green

Sweet Nectar Publishing

Invisible Me

To Zola and Skully Knuckles

Table of Contents

Acknowledgements

I am so thankful to my parents, Stan and Ramona for all of the love and support you've shown me and for having my back at all costs.

LaTora, thank you for giving me the best gift anyone has ever given me, my unborn daughter, Zola.

My brother, Josh, you've always motivated me without pushing, and for that, I thank you.

Susanna, my publisher, a special thanks to you for your guidance.

Introduction

Why am I still here? This question haunts me; lingering in my psyche. While at constant war with the thoughts in my head, and its allies' depression and anxiety, I find everyone experiences these things; but there are many who experience it on a much more debilitating level. There are many who have survived others they care about after watching them retreat to low places, or dark mental frequencies, if you will. Those vibrations shaped the world as I saw it, and to continue fighting it, or to rejuvenate my fight, all it took was love; a handful a people who were committed to seeing me through life, and wouldn't let me disappear. I can't even express my appreciation as I would like to, but I can do what they've all encouraged me to do, and that is pay it forward and tell my story. There may be someone who can relate, who needs this. I am more comfortable anxious and depressed. It feels better to hide from the world and let the bad in everything outweigh the good. Yet, what feels better isn't usually so. On the flip side, there is also freedom in going through it all, analyzing and expressing it constructively. Our emotions and experiences are real, we can't ignore them, yet they cannot make final decisions in our lives either. It would be foolish for me to act like I know or feel what anyone else has experienced. I can only tell you about me, because that is all I know. I'm only here to say you aren't alone. So, here I am…Enduring pain often brings about relief, just as light comes from darkness. So long as any soul is positively touched, by anything I have to offer, I shall continue to follow that path regardless. The point of nothing being perfect is so we are never too good for progress. As I feel frustration, it's a reminder to forever strive for better; not just for myself, but I need to always try, for any affect made on anything or anyone makes the world better. The point of oneness isn't sameness It's infinity. All possibilities, everything, instantly.
Illusions of death visiting, but all I recall is life intervened.
However you grow, the final product is a unique beauty.

Am I Selfish?

I'd like to learn to have fun
To enjoy the snow
the summer sun

I want to have a good time
One day, in the midst
of all that's on my mind

I'd love to know a sense of belonging
Even just a hint
so my soul is no longer longing

So, I'll try to learn to love
myself first,
Then I can give out enough.

Daily Affirmations

Take action, and walk my path with confidence
Just me, no need for a supportive audience
It's a world full of possibilities
Lead with faith; you'll be given the abilities.

Accept what makes me
Failure to do that which breaks me
Create abundance and fulfillment for myself
My happiness brings others joy and good health.

Combat depressions and anxiety with study
Practice
But first... meditating quietly.

Love Is It

I like to be smiled at
so, I'll grin for a while back
A gesture, a connection
Transcending dialects

I can't do life all by myself
I'll be there... if you ask
Not to say you owe me
To see half full in a glass

I won't judge you
because I don't want a trial
We all hold darkness
I cannot walk your mile

If I cause you suffering
Humble me, I'm ashamed
I need to learn and change
Our clashing's not in vain.

Rose

Love the rose
blooming through the concrete
In a midnight comfort zone
Conceiving to let light concede
It still contorts home
Thorns to bite and sting
So let it be

Product of the environment
and cannot leave
Learned from the cactus
Exhibit growth
Yet, not the fastest
Against an axis
Taking what's given

Allies blow with the wind
Same as sustained tactics
Little of worth
Drops of water
Scream
Use it
Infertile earth
it seems
but isn't useless

It rides out
the heat and cold
No doubt, it'll flourish
The rose yet beholds
Only love can nourish.

Blue Moon

I ask the universe, what's next?
Do you need me? I'm vexed.
Either I'm waiting, or I'm wasting;
Let me know, I can't rest!
Is it all in vain?
Shall I lift the weighted plate off my chest
or, take what's given
Be complacent with my placement?
I never knew what to do if I had three wishes
I just want to have paid my dues
or show me to the dishes
If preparation is the key
can you show me to the kitchen?
Don't let me invent the engine
and someone else go the distance.
I never knew what to do if I had three wishes
I just want to have paid my dues
or show me where to dig in
If preparation is the key
I'm ready to listen
Don't let me invent the engine
and it's never driven.
I ask the universe, what's next?
Do you need me? I'm vexed.
Waiting is wasting;
Let me know, I can't rest!
Is it all in vain?
Can I lift the weighted plate up off my chest
I appreciate what's given
but complacence doesn't place me at that next step.

Personalities Border-lined

A full phone, and no one to contact
I keep exploding, hoping no one bombs back
Trouble coping, and wasting away
Just to get up usually takes me the day
Hypochondriac aching for pain, like
The sun's out and I'm duct taping the panes
Getting love to give out a closed act
Apologies meaning nothing post attack
Though dealing with demons has its perks
The high helps so the low doesn't hurt
Depression and pressure ease the fear of the dirt
Repressions just a vector leading me from this Earth.

Quick Sand

The world's black hole...
Will I become free?
After a while or so
will the depths allow recovery?
It grabbed ahold, pulling me under
Sleek and slow it goes
Quick sand knows suffering
Throwing tantrums
Quickening the worst
A flowing mansion
The bottom dispersed
Eyes at the sun
I lean back and relax
Finding my abyss does the same thing back
Stray down a strange road
They say silence is golden
but I'll never get that halo
Not invited where they go,
I guess I'll just lay low
Taught to never follow
and always say no
So, I lead myself
like a stray, down a strange road
Met some smiles the other day
Not sure where they went
Could use a friend
Being different creates hatred
Haven't done much right
That's hard to take in
I'd love a hand in my fight
If they could take it.

Ranting and Raving

Are my long locks too feminine
My long beard to scraggly
Do I offend you,
Expressing the ancient African in me?
Or, is it the brown skin, why you're mad at me
And why is it, only my light-skinned kin
win in life's pageantry?
Does this also explain my skills
and useful mental faculties?

My apologies for ranting
but this is so sad to me
We all have our judgment on topics
and truths to which we just won't listen
An ideal of a perfect world
that certain others can't live in.

I can't find the reasons
It seems I don't fit in
I don't understand why we learn
there's an 'us' and a 'them'
Why does everything that's ever happened
in this world come back again
The depressing cycles and life patterns
I can't suspend.... Let alone end.

Advice

She told me, leave that zone of comfort

Whatever you're hiding from, confront it!

Whatever mask you wear

Get from under

I wonder

Why my angels care

Why I just disconnect into me

But in listening to their tough love

I'm freed instantly.

Maybe I'm Crazy

Is there a reason why daily tragedies are so sad to me?

Gradually becoming numb to every human causality

Natural is so vile; simplicity is out of style

Learn to lie, cheat and smile; work should be a pile

Is it I, or is the world suffering from insanity

Placing the blame on me seems better for humanity.

Whispers of Conscience

They call me
Assuring, I'll still be a being
when I'm dust.

They whisper to me
Righteousness...liberation
I hear them saying, "fight for this"
I ask to see the light
More truth and lies come
Easy way to learn
You can't just lie dumb.

Ignorance is bliss, but knowledge frees me
Truth is telling truths, ain't so easy.

Our ancestors, they follow us
We are them, again allowed touch
to live enticed in your world
and enlighten it.

Let it give light to you
Realize that since we are all dying
we should love each other like it.

I don't know very much but I am conscious
I am one with you all, I love you all.

Lost Youth

I threw rocks at the soldiers who oppressing me
Pa never worked, Ma stresses fees
No food, education, or tools to set me free
Death lingers but it won't get the best of me

No bread at night; I am bred to die
Role models and loved ones out of sight
I've lost it all; can't sleep at night
What is peace?
I've been bred to fight

Hard to trust when the law is made by thugs
They shot my brother down; called it 'war on drugs'
All I could get was cheap candy to fill me up
I'll make it home, ain't running out of luck

No bread at night; so I'm bred to die
Role models and loved ones alike
All out of sight
I've lost it all; can't sleep at night
What is peace?
I've been bred to fight.

Patrick or Patricia

I'll be here, as long as you need to cover your pain
When the paint's done blurring your face
Can I know your real name?
No need for details you're trying to forget
Remember you and all you love
to get you through these moments.

Conversing with a friend, I'd say we're really close
One of those, actually...
I've known longer than most.

Patrick or Patricia, I can't remember,
Let's call'em Pat
Finally, we get to the subject we always meant to.

Pat said, "I wanna quit; I'm beginning' to lose it,
gonna choose to end it soon."
I said, "Yo, Pat I can't lie
I can sense the gloom, no need for an interview
they medicated me
I still wake up and don't leave the room."

Our eyes locked, it was the look
Chills overtook
Pat knew my plight, but was ready to die
Why, oh why?

I told Pat, "Your wounds, I can't heal
Fight a little longer, I'll hike wit' you up this hill
Even when heading down the abyss
and you're too lonely still
It's best being alone together
Clowns masked on walking stilts."

I'll be here, as long as you need to cover your pain
When the paint's done blurring your face
Can I know your real name?
No need for details you're trying to forget
Remember you and all you love
to get you through these moments.

$$$

I used to think you were good for me

Now I know better

I still need you

Why control my efforts?

Brothel

He waits outside the brothel, gaze set to the sun

Out walks a brother, a smirk to say he had some fun

Urges set to scuffle, but wait… his lover comes

The look upon her face was one, glad he hadn't run

Heads turn to watch them, hand in hand down the street

After putting her to sleep

Day's spent thinking of the promises he'd keep

Of the love she needed, that he could never bring

Stare stuck behind her, wanting beneath the sheets

The waterbed reminds him, maybe he's in to deep

Help wanted ads never help; again, today he'll peek

Hoping to bring them out of depths

Closer to their peak

Or flee…

Cause she's okay, and can't hear a peep.

Oh... Just an Old Tree

Forever watching you all come and go

Many show love; some don't

We still allow you life, although you kill us off

Crowding us, using us, cutting us off

Not a problem, it's the cycle

For now, enjoy movement; I am idle

Remember to love, we are all living

Oh, and I am your roots, you are forgiven.

His Story's Grave

So many thoughts, too many ideas

No one here to talk, no one wants to hear

So many truths, so much which could help

But digging through histories' graves brings me hell

Maybe dark messages

But there's light to find in lessons

Maybe we should clean our messes

Before there's nothing left of us.

Norma Jean

Dear Norma, Tsunami floater
a rough life for ya
still a Stonehenge Boulder
Norma, Norma Jean
Smile at me please
Oh please my dear Norma Jean
Smile at me, would u please?

You've had to toss doves,
Left with questions, hands tossed up
Still, you're all love
Oppression and violence change sons to vile men
You stifle them
because still, you are all love
Norma, Norma Jean
Smile at me, please
Oh please, my dear Norma Jean
Smile at me, would u please?

Once a little girl, at peace in the field
Those days are missed, but gone still
You care so much, and it brought more pain
To keep on loving is the only way to gain
You've got some left
you swear you will cherish
You are loved and your love can never parish

Dear Norma, Tsunami floater
A rough life for ya
Still a Stonehenge Boulder
Norma, Norma Jean
Smile at me, would u please
Oh please my dear Norma Jean
Smile at me, would u please?

Lavender and Smoke
After night shift, it's always so clear
How so many of us are lonely, yet not alone here
We all have this hole,
How to make it whole is unclear
Growing up to find we're still lost
and can't do anything but steer;

Sometimes we crash, then have another go
In between, just take it all in
Lavender and smoke
Most time's, we'll laugh at the stories we show
Until then relax, with some lavender and smoke.

Black Cat

I'm just a black cat; a bit melanated at that
Not too many of my kind left; in my home, I stay kept
I know where I'm welcome, and where I'm not
Staying out of sight, crossing through dark spots
I know where there's fear; I know when there's not
I know where I'm a spectacle and where I'm god
I'm the same as the other cats, only a bit darker
I wish someone would tell them that
before they push my extinction any farther
Two as One...
As darkness approaches; sleep demons encroach us
Same lonely lost lotus; even with someone to hold us
We both have our own life's issue
I have no problem staying up all night with you;
Even if our bond is through the loneliness
We aren't blinded at our loneliest
Know I'm beside you to go through this
Even to tune in to our music
Rock 'n' roll with it...
We both have our own life's issue
I have no problem staying up all night with you;
Two souls lost, wandering together; better than one
Partners to endure the weather we could never see come
We both have our own life's issue
I have no problem staying up all night with you;
One way, or another, with each other we'll see it through
Find the Good...
Growing around lying, stealing, jealousy and killing
Learning hatred, because loving things is silly
Negative energy can be a filler
Positivity is fulfilling.

25

Free to Be

What could I possibly have for her?
She accepts measly offerings
Attached with more hurt.

What could she see in me?
The mirror doesn't reflect so easily
Vehemently, I don't let go
Poor her!

She can't see feasibly my former
Asking for a coroner
Holding on
But I know, she should be free to be.

Gods pet

Why can I not leave this place?
Got to pee, got to pace
Where you at; why'd u leave me?
Been forever; you're back, actin like you don't see me
I appreciate the fake food and poison water
Uncalled for discipline, only makes this world harder
I want my instincts, I want fun
I want my energy, I am sun!

God and I are friends, I know I'm not his pet
The people reading me his pamphlets say...
Act right and good you'll get
I followed the rules; swear to God I do
But honestly, it's not that cool being Gods pet
It's not that cool being Gods pet
Even at my best, it's really not that cool being Gods pet

In a world of confinement, can't go free 'til they let you
Mad at every little peep you leak
You'd swear they're out to get you
Lying to get their way, then give you the scraps
Stay in line and you might get a 'lil' p
God and I are friends, I know I'm not his pet

The people reading me his pamphlets say
"Act right and good you'll get"
I followed the rules; swear to God I do
But honestly, it's just not that cool being Gods pet
It's not that cool being Gods pet
I was mostly at my best
but still, it was not that cool being Gods pet

I am God, God is me; I believe in energy
It set me free. I am the sun; Anointed one's agree
For Christ's sakes I am love; with the light I can see
All of us beings, and things alike
Constantly being and becoming
We all always will be.

From Over Here

They can't understand why I sway
I kind of do...And don't
Hope they stay from over here
Away from where I'm watching the bonds,
laughter, and cheers
all the support, progress, and careers;

But, I'm over here, a bit awkward and weird
Am I weird because I'm lonely
or because that's where lonely steers?
Not doing too much, 'til the foggy path clears
I'll let y'all keep the vibes up in your circle from over here

It's so vivid, so clear, when surrounded by peers
Out there on his pier, there's only one who peers
From over here, water fills my ears
Flows of conversations and communion I revere
I can't join in, naw; not from over here

I don't want to see this damn man
forever standing in my mirror
Why show that off;
Who has time for self-consciousness and fear?

My mind is nowhere near clear;
I just need to watch from over here.

Heresy

Ever feel like a total heretic, mere edits

Completely distorting the whole message

Fear of ethics and morals

Deemed alright to be overstepped

You know what's wrong and right

You forgive, and don't forget

Meditation

The coldest the wind blows

All are asleep

One toad still croaks

But, he ain't lost a beat.

A Plea for Peace

When is the last time peace and freedom
coexisted across the world?
Why have leaders and people
always been so addicted to war?
The power, what is it for?
Why in the world can't we get rid of war?
I just looked into the eyes of a child of war
Last thing on her mind was
they live well below poor.
Sisters fighting with brothers
to keep their people's lives
No father, and her mother
just doesn't seem right
Don't be fooled
There's no rules to contain violence
Women and children die, towns become silent
Hear bullets and bombs
like she's right beside them
An adolescent...
who knows her future looks shortsighted.
When is last time peace and freedom
coexisted across the world?
Why have leaders and people
always been so addicted to war?
The power, what is it for?
Why in the world can't we get rid of war?
For black males, this is a police state
They militarize riots
when they're wrong for Pete's sake
Innocent people killed out of fear
or, is it hate?

31

Through blurred lines we can't see clear
a remake of segregation is currently here
Housing, schools, businesses and politics
Just ain't fair; nobody cares;
this ain't nothing a representative is trying to hear
Not the half white representation we have in there
Get past emotions so facts can steer
There's a modern day slavery
Poison in the air
Disease in the food, oppression is in motion
but genocides are near.
When is last time peace and freedom
coexisted across the world?
Why have leaders and people
always been so addicted to war?
The power, what is it for?
Why in the world can't we get rid of war?

Take Me

I get to remove the residue and lay down next to u

Interrupt the rest in you, just to see the rest of you

What a messed up two, in hell with the best of views

Impaled and destitute, and worst of all, rescue proof

The lessons lose, I've found where I'm happiest

Although, I don't know what happy is

You lead me to it with savviness

Understanding my silence, without asking it.

Apology Letter

I don't mean to cause you pain
As if all efforts are lost, in vain
as if, at no cost and any length
Can you touch the heart, even breach the veins.

I yearn to stop your worry
Concern, as the glare in your eyes get blurry
is appreciated, words encouraging
Never too late, never too early.

I hope I can ease your hurting
as you watch your loved one swerving
Along their path, foundation not so sturdy.

It's not in your hands, but your love is working
the feel of tension is concerning
I'm pulling back, without discerning.

My weakness is connections
With your patience, I am learning
Here's a hug back, lasting and firmly.

Sleep

You look so peaceful now

Watching your deeply breathe

Never really awake

Sleep walking to beat that

Your heartbeat says, life feels like a race

It's in vain to keep speeding

Trust me!

I got the drive

But we may arrive, while you're sleeping.

Mojave

If struggle shapes us
We crave the hard way
Lovers in the Mojave
Delusions of destiny
As fates' call awaits
Dune recipe
The deserts' sweet taste
Just us two
Forever...always

Lovers from the Mojave
Starry sky
Yet, no substance to sustain us
We'll try
Although, the Sun makes no way for luck
We can get through
And forget what they all say

Lovers of the Mojave
If struggle shapes us
Let's take the hard way
Lovers of the Mojave.

The Calls

There's nothing like that call when you've almost landed
your fall Ended like that's all folks, cliché like that's all she
wrote;

Stuck so far from hope. There's nothing like that call from
a friend to check in;

The surprising tug of the bungee cord; I forgot how often I
sky dive, and how I love and abhor that the divine gave me
a buddy who always brings a parachute;

The little angels of mine who brought the oxygen tankful's
and life jackets, of whom I hate, but yes still, I am so
grateful;

There's nothing like it; like the call that wakes me from
that deep sleep. When I just knew I wouldn't hear a peep,
and no one would notice my exit door creep;

That voice rings just perfectly. Calling me back from my
illusionary paradisiac. And, I realize, that life's worth it to
me.

Dear, Learn to Love You

Life is beautiful, yet still filled with much ugliness
But ugly has something of beauty right up under it;
Hard to grasp why she continues suffering
Blessings like on lay-away, such slow buffering
She could never truthfully say, 'I'm into loving me'
Sink down an abyss at any point suddenly;

Life is beautiful, yet still filled with much ugliness,
But ugly has something of beauty right up under it;
Darling, you are gonna see better days
Falling karma will finally okay your earned raise
Stay here on earth, Love, the pain won't remain
All the demons engrained, will someday be erased;

Life is beautiful, yet still filled with much ugliness
But ugly has something of beauty right up under it;
When you love you, you can love free
And your love for me will be so lovely
Your love for the world will relieve
Any poverties and dis-ease,
Even during your hardest trials
Your mental can stay pleased.

What If?

What if you knew me
like you use to?

Would the love still be there;
Is it foolproof?

What if I knew you
like I once thought?

Wouldn't I retreat
when I see you distraught?

What if we never had
each other by the throat?

Would the passion still
pass through us so?

Endless Horizons

Unsure of what's in store

The grumble inside yells for more

The hunger keeps me driving

Around the fools' gold towards the silver lining

From sunset 'til the suns rising

My eyes rest on endless horizons

Easing the strain of time

As I mind the tense-less silence.

In Still Water

In still water
Is there a pattern to these old ripples?

Instill water
Mathematically the flow seems so simple.

Unknown Colors

Infinite life

Shedding intimate light

Like stars into the night

Fretting the undiscovered

I can't help but wonder

About all the unknown colors.

Nomad

Given a poisoned well
Forcing me to go mad
Crops from hell
Dehydration make a nomad.

Confusing white lies
My mentality needs to be re-routed
Rebooting the mind's eye
is a journey, I keep moving.

Going with the flow
Sun or snowing
All good things to know
when comes more rowing.

Given a poisoned well
Forcing me to go mad
Crops from hell
Dehydration make a nomad.

Turning Tombs

The turning tombs

Give unnerving blooms

And, growing room

Conquering fear

Then returning to.

The Flow

What if I'm tied up when the tide's down

And miss my perfect chance

What if I'm tied down when the tides up

Reminiscing worsened plans

Need to stop lying, when I lie down

I've come to miss my dreams

Dying to be dyed, and deceived my very being.

Emotions lead by a Heart

Power
Emotion
Passion evoking
Masses controlling
Passive yet potent;
Feelings,
they fluctuate from the floor
to the ceiling
Creating a movie scene
constantly reeling
Damaging
yet healing;
Can be strength
as well as Achilles
As we go deeper
and more in
Tendency's sway
Constant morphing;
At times the darkest nights
linger 'til the morning
Nothing's ever perfect
Constant mourning
Live life with storms
and rough waters;
Hardships and tribulations
slowly become harder
Coming off the bench
can be a rough starter
Faith and will
will take me much farther.

Basics

Go through the lies and the truth

Peep the disguise in the proofs

Blueprint life's movements

The rudiment like rules.

Leap of Faith

At any moment I could die

Wonder what I might find

At any moment, I could fly now

Wonder what difference it makes

Jumping high down.

Happy Questions

To what extent does this thing called happiness exist?
Does it come with personal checklists
and moments we are free to exit?

Is it mixed in with the lessons, and other sorts of testing?
Could it be more like a spectrum
comparable to our last experiences?

Does it even matter
or is the matter dark in all seriousness?
Is there something sick and twisted
about our pleasure senses?

Hedonists, who look upward for restraints;
place admissions
Rather than standing in the mirror
being honest with the misses.

The pride in bellowing our hits, and stolen third base visits
Our humanness betrayed by base senses
Or, is that what makes us so?

More importantly, is that what makes us go?
Happy, you shouldn't question, sometimes
It only hurts to know.

Wake up Call

We all will pass, like walking by

But I hope you wake up, before you die

All our life, we've been passed these lies

Glad to be awake, what it takes to survive.

Disillusioned

Will we ever be different?

Better than better seems distant

Weathered through the weather

Withering, yet optimistic;

Dolling up the bruises

As if, adopting mystics

Affecting what's beneath

But, we believe our optics vision;

The effect on what's beneath comes out

If we only listen.

What For?

What is all this for; is it a test
If so, then what's in store?
Should I give the rest of what's left of my core
Or, Just keep stepping and pressing
'Til I'm sore; but what for?
Is this for my pride which we've been taught to hide
Told to love, yet be tough and neglect our insides?

Now, Where...
Where do we go from here?
Only forward...
When stagnancy proceeds toward digression
Slowly, let go of fears
Still, no direction
Appears the same question.

In my mind
I wonder where in the dark the stars align
The blind leading those in a bind
Could there be a better curse?
Swerve, seeing the signs
still forever serve
Forgotten progress...Lost steps
Paved wilderness.

Dilemma

It's Hard to talk to me
So, I usually stay in, or walk around awkwardly
Like I'm the only kid in my class most days
Trying to learn how the world's woes might pass
and get passed our old ways;

Come, please walk with me
Instead of just watching and doing your job
while working hard, hardly
I know, if we really lived and loved
we'd be and feel so great;

Dying to earn an explanation for us
taking the same highly traveled roadways
Nobody can tell me why we are here, or what for
And, I could die tonight
with no chance to look more.

Cloudless

Storm, no cloud and blue sky

The norms that keep us down will soon die

Mourning these Knights, on a tour of the night

Storm, no clouds, blue skies.

Angelic Abysmal; Light and Heavy

Death means nothing

Souls being molded clay

Patterned, formed and shaped

Just a thing

It will wither and lay

Get thrown away

Be abused and used

And do some things great.

It must be so quiet in a Vacuum

I can't find a right place
So I just pace and pace
I can't wait
So I just race the chase

A one man riot in a black room
I bet it's so quiet in a vacuum
Noise flashing like bright lights
Distractions blinding and bind tight

Here's where connections meet a sad doom
It must be so quiet in a vacuum
It's a void
Where there's no need to avoid

Here, there's a voice for my dark matters choice
In need of a ploy to lose the sad tunes
Finding myself too comfortable where the bad looms
A lone man riots in a black room
It must be so quiet in a vacuum.

Rage

It all empties as rage

A quiet storm

Driving me super sane

An envious game

Like the rose and thorn

While the two are the same

Hoping to hide

With beauty the stains

Eloping to the eye

Yet, the name remains.

Trying for an Explanation

Words can't explain it
The anger, and frustration
Like an obsessive child facing rearrangement
Holding the monster within the basement
As the attic paces;

Channel it, avoid attacks, invasions
Then the pain manifests physically
With no restraint
I'm told it's happening mentally
Their one in the same;

I ask, "Can sanity make me insane?"
Maybe it's a hint to leave
When I'm going against the grain
This may not be fit for me.

Find Me

Rejecting the sweet words, whispered kindly
Constantly at war, facing behind me
Wrong direction to find where the signs lead
But a great path, if you want to live I.V.ed
I don't feel like a missing piece to any puzzle
When lost, instantly loss of all struggle
I use to fight it, now it's a place of comfort
Anytime I find the world, that's the place I run for;

From purgatory to hell; In need of momentum's swing
Troubled, not doing well, can't even begin to think
Unsure where my angel fell, then in it sinks
First key to escaping jail, I have to find me;

I'm empty, really can't find much
Searching, and at the bottom; it's repeating I'm stuck
Words don't want to leave, containing real emotion
Not much I see, deserving real devotion
Sometimes I forget to breathe, upset when I realize
Mostly because when I heed, I still don't feel life.

More Ranting and Raving

Profitable wars, prophetic lies
Lending a mosh pit of gore and burning bush fires
Different parties same melodic lines
Tempting cameras, phones, and wires
Skewing employment, with slaves still under whip
Still picking up vagrants for prisons cotton-picks
Traded for a few more bosses and no resources
Latent is the oppressive institutions used as torches
Those who protect just need military reinforcements
Serving those who have always had their voices
But no more long days in the field, and deaths unanswered
Well, only for the most part, like chemo shuns cancer
Society looks sick, but we are sure fighting it
No more colored seating, and our schools are mighty fit
Teaching us respect of self, and deep thought
Promoting those whose allegiance can't be bought
Send humanitarians off to be fought
Giving livelihood to those who need help and sought
With a constitution as sarcastic as the latter
We find ourselves in the same God-Damn battle
Even with the saved venom from the snake that rattles
The second strike kills from society's adder
I should digress from my hatred of home
Magnify my lens of the world, poor left alone
as the wealthy have plans unfurl
Everyday people, living in war zones
Kidnapping, raping, and killing all their own
Chrome in a boys' hands reaping what his leader sows
Mold children to form a race of man
with no conscious of its own
Agree to meet demands regardless if we know
that it's the devil's contract buying out our souls.

These Walls

These walls could use a fresh coat
Plus some manners
You crowd me
Never let me go meander
There's a lot I need to let go
Maybe, I'll get the answers
Pounding paneling holed
Doesn't help lower standards.

High hopes, with lost faith
Turns to destiny costs fate
Maybe it's just a long phase
A habit of wearing the wrong face
Looking for the bright side
Could make for a long day
While there's a solar eclipse
Pausing in my hallway.

What's In Comes Out

The days don't change
Blurred and so strange
Soul chained,
Mind of a super-nova Cained.

Disabled, crutched and behind the scenes
The heart following emotions schemes
Unnerved by all the commotion, the screams
A macrocosm of what's bellowing beneath.

Steer Clear

Veering is easy, staring in the rear view
Listening so intently, but can't even hear you
Intrigued and teased by evil residing in good
Reminding Zen of its old defining blood
My love, as unconditional as my hate
Like the being and its fetus cycling a sideways eight;

A dilated space needed for this back and forth
Due to minding
Dilapidated traces of me is what you're asking for
If you find me;

Withholding means destruction
Remolding and reconstruction
Seething defeats the function
Leading to release combustion.

All Bottled Up

That bottle got most I know
Some still walkin... Some comatose
Bust it on edge
Jagged to the throat
Answers what's at the end
Shattered type of hope
Drowned it out
Bound around a bout
Facing the mirror
Stricken, and fouled out

That bottle got most I know
Some walkin...Most comatose
Bust it on edge
Jagged to the throat
Is this my end?
Dear God, don't let me go.

Personalities

Alluding me once again
Thought I had a win, but I'm
Hardened, covered in sin, hiding
Darkness from within;

How long are we staying together this time?
Usually I'm in the wrong
when saying it's time
But I can't hide, fearing I'll lose my mind
or a toe may cross this mine;

Right angel on the shoulder
Whispering...
The fallen one got left in me
and livin' free.

Am I?

I've got to break this
I'm out of blankets
No more cover-ups
No space to color up the basement;

Piling up adjacent
To its origin in the attic
I come face to face with...
Am I no more than just an addict?

A Round in a Ring

A fit of fears, taut taunting, no, teasing
Consumed, obsolete obesity
Looms faith in stability, hopes of decency
Amidst hostility amongst those frequencies
Give in is a given, that's so easy
While a round in a ring can be so freeing
The sounds and the scenes can be so deceiving
but a round in a ring can be so freeing
Squared up
Toe to toe
both bleeding
Maybe it's about pride
but no pleading
Could be about the high
who knows
our souls are greedy
I'm not alone in those who come competing
Give in, is a given, that's too easy
While a round in a ring can be so freeing
The sounds and the scenes can be so deceiving
but a round in a ring can be so freeing.

Let's Talk

To be honest destroys too much
To lie does the same
Neither voices the struggles
we have in an exchange;

Neither settles the troubles
resting on our brains
It takes both truth and deception
to wash out all stains.

Devil

Give him something to eat and have it spit at my feet
Give him fifty feet to be put on a leash
Storming back as soon as dust settles
I can only be so nice to the devil;
Loaned my home, forced to roam
Help, to be stoned and get thrown bones
Broken, wondering why I'm not a rebel
Going the distance to be nice to the devil;
Shot my son, gave my wife cancer
Gave me drugs and guns; God's number, never answered
Shouting love, to be ousted and heckled
Still got nothing but a smile for the devil;
Tried to offer me a deal, said I couldn't pass
Told me, I just had to kneel, I told him, "Kiss my ass"
Sorry to be so brash, you've been heating my kettle
Just right to give hell to the devil;

My emotions keep me trapped, I need my heart to lead
My mind's held hostage, it's kind of hard to leave
All plugged up, it's getting hard to breathe
Need to recharge my batteries
These thoughts of blasphemy must be pious
Caught up, have to flee the silence
Papyrus tactfully raising riots
I can shut my eyes, forgetting the sirens
Brain locked in auto-pilot; emotions want to bust through
Heart beating through the body;
tellin' me, "Man, this isn't you"
Could be rage or depression, a phase or a weapon
A face so deceptive remains so no one is let in
I'm Better Elsewhere, sorry I stole the spot of a first-born
Coming out of nowhere, stealing only the earth form

Sensitive and phlegmatic, cryptically foreign
You never knew the real me, why the search for him
My cursed fortune knows no boundaries
Effective immediately, when you found me;
I'll understand if you let me go
Trust me I know
It ain't easy to have me home
They told me, it's the wrong direction,
I even had the thought
Staring at my reflection, analyzing the costs of regrets
Should haves and ought'
Often neglecting me, wreaking wrought
Can't trust my thoughts, I'm down to my last wit
I spot traffic, stop, head opposite adamant
Why teach me such patience
To see the days anew
They allege we are caged, is it so or made true
If it is written can we be indifferent
and remove that page too
Am I expected to listen and not to rage through?
How does one love, as I state I hate you?
As I'm craving paid dues, not deserving of shit
Then making a way through all not pertinent
Submerged in emotions, cycling the giving and the get
Surging a commotion, hiding and missing experience.

Evolution Seems Stuck

Broken radars, undetected deep stuff
Things we don't ever want to think of
Evolution seems stuck
Obtrusive is all we've become
Ignoring deaths with our feet up
Helping the hands of these demons
Evolution seems stuck
Oblivious to how far we've come

All we know is, fight for what we desire
Promote peace, and create an empire
Distracted and numb so we never inquire
Choirs of women and children shout in fires
The whole world is in dire need
The onlookers of hell watch silently
Working for a machine that operates violently
Makes it hard to meet my maker, when it's time to leave

Butterflies urging me to come with them
To shed the cocoon and run with wind
The grass shows me, I'll grow
Regardless how slow I go, within
What good is there in fearing the inevitable?
I'm holding on, tip-toeing towards letting go
Slipping slowing, ready to experience the fall
If only flight was one of my defaults.

Living A Lie

Death comes from truth here
It's a mess, an abstruse fear
Obtuse, yet so obtrusive
Unused truth isn't useless
Hence, honesty breeds polarity
Sense's becoming common is a rarity
Understanding exists variably
Seems to be scared of free
We limit it
The highest love is condition-less and infinite
We oppress ourselves to a partial side of intimate
As an instrument
I can only play the notes given
Hoping to create the combinations
Of those that couldn't fit in
Nothing in the ear would you hear as a lie
Even the contradictions could appear to be right
Whose to negate with proof otherwise?
Why should I hide?
For light will imbibe; I'll never rest, if it's kept inside.

Moccasin Reach

Reach out
Don't explain why
See what they're about
When you're in bouts and the time is right
Reached out
Only to find
I'm about to see
what I'm really about this time;

Confront a moccasin
Just to mock it's sins
Being one in the same
attracting opposites
Studying kamikazes
loving all that's costly;

Reached out
to see what the seas 'bout
The cliff behind
My feet feel the breeze now
Flying or falling
well what do you seek out
In the way of ourselves
Receiving beat downs
Water fall and catch me
Post karma's sweet sound;

Confront a moccasin
In hopes of fostering
We are one in the same
Attracted opposites
Was a kamikaze
knowing what it will cost me;

Reach now
for the lessons instilled
Teach how
the blessings willed
At the feet now
of my pedestal
Break it down
Unknown if man ever will.

When I'm Hiding Please don't Seek

Burrowed in my little hole
Protect me from the warmth, and the cold
Down here is dark, territory unknown
Around where no souls roam
Hanging with friends all alone
Still I feel safe here
You can't find my entrance or escape
So I'll stay here;

Disappeared within my shell
Don't come close, I can't help myself
I like the blackness, it's comforting
My awareness is of nothing but me
Maybe it didn't help but I feel safe here
Really not sure what you want
So I'll stay here;

Recycling through my abyss as well as neurosis
Yearn for love, expectations out of focus
Unconditional... omit the running amiss component
But as of now, I just want to hide for a moment
Selfish I know but I feel safe here
I kind of want to get out
But, I'll just stay here;

Would You Come Down for a visit?
I don't really think anyone knows me
Even when I'm hugged, I'm not really held closely
Lately in life, I've been feeling fairly lowly
It's easy standing up,
but would some stoop down to hold me?
Stares and paths sometimes cross so coldly
No wonder there are billions of people, and someone
could feel lonely;

Lately in life when you feel fairly lowly
Say, "I can't stand it, can you stoop down and hold me?"
No solace, just pain walking sole-less solely
Developing the feeling of becoming soulless slowly
When that's what you call feeling fairly lowly
We just need for someone
to stoop down with us in holding.

Mother of Snakes

May we sit together?
I'd like a perspective inward
One that comes untethered
You see, I'm sick and residing inwards
Where the spectrum ends at specter
I'll release all that hinders me
From reminding what's worth remembering

I know that you'll sit with me
It's just a matter of the snake hunt
I never admired slithering
for she left me with two scrapes once
Yet, I know we owe to sit
and keep each other company
Then I can run from you, just as you'll run from me
Enduring pain often brings about relief
Just as light comes from darkness.

www.ingramcontent.com/pod-product-compliance
Lightning Source LLC
LaVergne TN
LVHW021542080426
835509LV00019B/2799